T0209144

ARMORUP

PUTTING ON THE FULL ARMOR OF GOD

RAY A. FRANCIS, SR.

WESTBOW
PRESS®
A DIVISION OF THOMAS NELSON
& ZONDERVAN

WestBow Press books may be ordered through booksellers or by contacting:

WestBow Press
A Division of Thomas Nelson & Zondervan
1663 Liberty Drive
Bloomington, IN 47403
www.westbowpress.com
1 (866) 928-1240

Interior Image Credit: Christian Foulcard

Scripture quotations marked NLT are taken from the Holy Bible, New Living Translation, Copyright © 1996, 2004, 2015 by Tyndale House Foundation. Used by permission of Tyndale House Publishers, Inc., Carol Stream, Illinois 60188. All rights reserved.

ISBN: 978-1-9736-9360-4 (sc)
ISBN: 978-1-9736-9359-8 (hc)
ISBN: 978-1-9736-9361-1 (e)

Library of Congress Control Number: 2020910247

Print information available on the last page.

WestBow Press rev. date: 6/10/2020

ARMORUP

PUTTING ON THE FULL ARMOR OF GOD

For Pamelyn, Ray (RJay), Justin, Alexandra, Milan, Kyndal and Lauryn. Thank you for being my motivation to ArmorUp daily.

For my mother, Claudia, whose love and support has helped me to become the man that I am.

For my dad, Wallace, who has been an example to me for how a man should ArmorUp daily.

For Andre, my Hornet brothers and the brothers of the ArmorUp football league. Your encouragement, support and prayers mean more to me than you know.

What Do We Mean When We Say ArmorUp?

Putting on our armor is a responsibility, a right, and a privilege! As Christians, Paul commands us to "Put on all of God's armor" (Ephesians 6:11). Athletes know and understand they have a uniform to wear that identifies which team they're on and have the proper protection for the sport. Christianity has a uniform, and God designed it to protect us on the battlefield. We are, therefore, responsible to wear our armor daily to "Fight the good fight for the true faith" (1 Timothy 6:12).

It is also our right as Christians to have a set of armor. Every player on a team is given a uniform and the equipment necessary to compete. But it's only effective if we use it! You must put it on! It's a privilege because we get to put it on! Remember the feeling of putting on your first team uniform? How proud and excited you were to represent the team, your family, and your teammates? This is how we should feel daily as we prepare for battle. ArmorUp is designed to remind us that we should suit up daily and prepare our hearts and minds for the spiritual battle we will face.

As a man, it is our right to do so. The Lord gave Adam a job before He gave him a wife and family. Our job is to armor up and defend our family and walk in a way that glorifies the Lord! Your wife deserves a man who loves the Lord, serves the Lord, and will put her needs and the family's needs before his. By Armoring Up, we accept this responsibility gladly and boldly to live a life before our family and friends that pleases the Lord and points others to Him. Our daughters need to see a man who is an example of who they should aspire to marry. Our sons deserve to see a man they should aspire to be like. By Armoring Up, we are committing to be that man!

Please pray for guidance as you follow this ministry and trust the Lord to help you ArmorUp daily and fight the battle in a way that brings Him glory and draws others to Him! Don't just suit up, ArmorUp!!!

Armor Up

Good morning, brothers!

"Put on all of God's armor so that you will be able to stand firm against all strategies of the devil" (Ephesians 6:11).

This is our foundational Scripture! We have to be ready for battle daily. An athlete doesn't go into a game, nor does a soldier go into battle without the proper gear on. They also have to have a game plan. Why do we choose to go through a day without being properly suited or without a plan?

And, this is not just a one-time thing! We have to prepare for battle daily. We need to spend time in prayer and devotion. We have to take time with the Lord so that He may speak to us. Also, we need to pray for others, especially the families we lead! We need to fellowship with other believers, our teammates, to draw strength from one another and provide encouragement and support as we move forward with the Lord. Let's invite the Lord into all that we do! Let's get battle-ready, brothers! A new day begins, and the enemy is on the attack! Don't just wake up and suit up...

#ArmorUp!!!

Fix Your Thoughts

Good morning, brothers!

"You will keep in perfect peace all who trust in You, all whose thoughts are fixed on You!" (Isaiah 26:3).

Being an imperfect person and living in an imperfect world leads to imperfect occurrences. Those imperfections can cause major stress in our lives. In the Lord, we can find peace. Not just peace, but perfect peace! We just need to trust in Him and focus our thoughts on Him.

Our thoughts can be distractions from what God planned for us. In the world today, people are always talking about "living in their truth." Actually, they have mistaken truth for reality. Just because it's real doesn't make it the truth! The world's mindset has changed. We have to fix our mindset on the Lord.

Things happen so quickly in life, and we try to control them. We will lose control. Why not give up control instead of losing it? When we yield control to the Lord, we find a peace we can't explain. We find assurance that all will work for our good. We find certain victory!

Storms will come. We have to keep our vision fixed on the One Who is constant in the storms of change. In Him, we will find and live in peace.

Reality changes. The Lord is the same yesterday, today, and forever! Fix your mind on the Lord! Walk in the Truth today!

#ArmorUp!!!

We Have an Advocate

Good morning, brothers!

"My dear children, I am writing this to you so that you will not sin. But if anyone does sin, we have an Advocate who pleads our case before the Father. He is Jesus Christ, the One Who is truly righteous. He Himself is the sacrifice that atones for our sins—and not only our sins but the sins of all the world" (1 John 2:1-2).

The Lord desires for us to stay away from sin. However, in this war between spirit and flesh, we sometimes lose battles. Jesus came to wash away our sins. We who have come to Jesus know how to come back to the Lord when we stumble. We have to be a living example to those who are lost. If anyone wants to be free from sin, he must come to Jesus. Jesus is the One Who not only died for our sins; He also pleads our case before the Father.

Jesus is our Great Defense Attorney! Every time the devil stands before the Father to prosecute and accuse us, Jesus is there to plead our case. Also, because of Jesus' sacrifice, the Father sees us through bloodstained glasses, and we can be in His presence because of Jesus!

We are free to live the life He has called us to. What will we do with that freedom? How will we repay the One who paid it all for us? Let's choose to live a life pleasing and honoring to Jesus! We need to let our lights shine today! We are free!!!

#ArmorUp!!!

Be on Alert

Good morning, brothers!

"Stay alert! Watch out for your great enemy, the devil. He prowls around like a roaring lion, looking for someone to devour. Stand firm against him, and be strong in your faith. Remember that your family of believers all over the world is going through the same kind of suffering you are" (1 Peter 5:8-9).

We are on the same team and have the same opponent. This opponent is out to destroy us all! But we already have the victory! We are not fighting him for victory; we are fighting him FROM victory! Walk in the victory of Christ today!

This opponent studies us and knows which buttons to push to make us stumble and fall. We have to be alert and recognize his tactics. They are not new, but they are subtle. If we are not on our guard, they can trip us up. Let's not fall for his tricks or trust in our strength.

We must trust the Holy Spirit to guide us and follow His lead! Also, remember we don't have to go it alone. We have other believers who can encourage us and share their experiences with us. We are in this together!

#ArmorUp!!!

5
DAY

Do You Want Wisdom? Just Ask!

Good morning, brothers!

"If you need wisdom, ask our generous God, and He will give it to you. He will not rebuke you for asking" (James 1:5).

We have been taught by the world that wisdom is knowledge plus experience. James tells us that instead of trying to figure it out on our own or waiting for an experience, we should go directly to the Source. The Lord is always waiting for us to bring our needs to Him. He is ever-willing to supply our needs. However, when we bring our needs to Him, we must leave them there.

God is the End to ALL means! When He is our Source, there is no need to look any further. If we choose to try other means, then we show God we don't trust Him, and He won't act on our behalf. We must strengthen our faith and learn that, "Anyone who wants to come to Him must believe that God exists and that He rewards those who sincerely seek Him" (Hebrews 11:6).

We can learn from the experiences of others and apply their lessons to our lives. Even better, why not learn from the wealth of knowledge and experience God has? Ask Him for wisdom and watch Him provide it. No need to shop around! Did Solomon get his wisdom from experience? No! He got it by asking the Lord for it! Let's go to the Source for our wisdom and not rely on our resources to get us there!

#ArmorUp!!!

How to Experience God's Peace (Part 1)

Good morning, brothers!

"Then you will experience God's peace, which exceeds anything we can understand. His peace will guard your hearts and minds as you live in Christ Jesus" (Philippians 4:7).

We all want God's peace. We know we will experience turmoil in this world, but we want God's peace in the midst of it. We can experience that peace that passes understanding, but there is a requirement.

When will we experience this peace? When we "don't worry about anything; instead, pray about everything. Tell God what you need, and thank Him for all He has done" (Philippians 4:6). We must change our mindset! Prayer and worry can't coexist! Peace has no place if worry is present! It's eviction time, worry! We have to make room for peace! Prayer needs the right roommate! It's time to clean house!

#ArmorUp!!!

Our Good Is Not Good Enough

Good morning, brothers!

"So letting your sinful nature control your mind leads to death. But letting the Spirit control your mind leads to life and peace. For the sinful nature is always hostile to God. It never did obey God's laws, and it never will. That's why those who are still under the control of their sinful nature can never please God" (Romans 8:6-8).

In and of ourselves, we can't please God. It's just that simple. Our good will never be good enough! We must surrender to the Lord.

The Holy Spirit wants to do what is pleasing to the Father. Our sinful nature only wants to satisfy itself. Pleasing God to the flesh is a means to that end! It will go along with God's will as long as it is convenient and leads to its satisfaction. We have to recognize when we have yielded to our flesh and repent! We must crucify this flesh and follow the Lord! We have to choose to follow the Holy Spirit. We can't compromise!

#ArmorUp!!!

DAY 8

Walk in the Light

Good morning, brothers!

"All who do evil hate the light and refuse to go near it for fear their sins will be exposed. But those who do what is right come to the light so others can see that they are doing what God wants" (John 3:20-21).

Light exposes. Light eliminates darkness. When it is focused, light can even cut and burn. Darkness hides, covers, and even blinds. Light allows us to see things as they really are.

Jesus is the Light of the world. He reveals things as they really are. He exposed the Pharisees' hypocrisy. He exposed the lifestyle of the woman at the well. He tells us of our sins and iniquity. His light can cut and burn away the sin that holds us back. He points us to the right path to follow. Are we choosing to walk in the Light today?

#ArmorUp!!!

How to Experience God's Peace (Part 2)

Good morning, brothers!

"I am leaving you with a gift—peace of mind and heart. And the peace I give is a gift the world cannot give. So don't be troubled or afraid" (John 14:27).

We all have thought that when we achieved a particular goal or reached a particular milestone in life, we would find peace waiting for us. How disappointing was it when we got there, and peace was nowhere to be found? We will not find peace in things or accomplishments. And, if we were to find peace in them, it wouldn't last.

Jesus is the Source of true, everlasting peace. The peace He gives us goes deep into the heart and mind. Worry and turmoil, circumstances, and situations can't reach the depths the Lord's peace reaches.

When we look to Him for guidance and direction, we find it, along with His peace. His peace gives us the calm to "endure suffering," as Paul instructs us in 2 Timothy 2:3. His peace reassures us when the world tells us to doubt. His peace passes all understanding. Thank you, Lord, for a peace that drives out fear and doubt and is everlasting!

No pill, person, possession, or position can give you the peace you find in Christ Jesus! Everything else leaves us feeling empty and wanting more. The more things we try, the emptier we feel. Jesus alone is enough! We need to put our trust in the One who knows exactly what we need, where we need it, and when we need it.

There is peace in submission to Him! Release the authority, the responsibility, and ordering of every detail to Him and watch what happens! If you desire peace, be still and let the Lord lead the way!

#ArmorUp!!!

Find Joy in Discipline

Good morning, brothers!

"No discipline is enjoyable while it is happening—it's painful! But afterward there will be a peaceful harvest of right living for those who are trained in this way" (Hebrews 12:11).

I don't know anyone who says they enjoy being disciplined. I remember the "growing pains of correction" from childhood. While it wasn't fun getting disciplined, I appreciate the man it has helped me become.

The same should apply to our spiritual growth and development. The Lord will correct us. It will not feel good, but it will benefit us in the long run. The Lord will guide us in the right way if we would just trust Him.

Let's benefit from God's wisdom and trust in His discipline. We know He loves us and wants the best for us. Why not allow Him to guide us through victory?

#ArmorUp!!!

There's Only One Way!

Good morning, brothers!

"Jesus told him, 'I am the Way, the Truth, and the Life. No one can come to the Father except through Me'" (John 14:6).

Mankind has tried to make its own way to heaven. We have allowed the devil to fool us into thinking we could be good enough to make it there on our merits. We have been fooled into thinking we don't have to live by God's rules or follow God's plan and can still find a way to heaven. Believing that will get us into the kingdom alright—the kingdom of hell!

Jesus is the perfect example of living God's way. There is no other way. We can't "get a pass." We won't get there by good behavior, good looks, or good deeds. Having a lot of money, giving to the poor, or being kind to those less fortunate won't cut it either. We must submit to the Lord and follow His pattern. There is a victory in submission! There is no other Way than Jesus! Let's follow Him today!

#ArmorUp!!!

How to Handle Difficulties

Good morning, brothers!

"In His kindness God called you to share in His eternal glory by means of Christ Jesus. So after you have suffered a little while, He will restore, support, and strengthen you, and He will place you on a firm foundation" (1 Peter 5:10).

Being a Christian doesn't make us exempt from difficulties. Storms will come. We will experience hard times. But, if we continue to look to Jesus, we will find restoration! God sends storms to test us. Storms are sent to remove some distractions. Storms are sent to move us closer to the Lord's will for our lives.

Thank God for the storms! Even better, thank God for His grace and mercy that restore us after the storms! Peter knew firsthand about Jesus' power during a storm. This same Jesus wants to calm the storms in our lives. Let's surrender the authority of our lives to Him!!!

#ArmorUp!!!

Have No Fear!

Good morning, brothers!

"For God has not given us a spirit of fear and timidity, but of power, love, and self-discipline" (2 Timothy 1:7).

When God commands us to do something, our reaction shouldn't be one of fear or timidity. If He calls us to it, He will equip us for it! Our faith in Him should cause us to respond positively. This Scripture attacks our excuse for having a defeatist attitude. If we are the Lord's, fear has no place in our lives.

Neale Donald Walsch says fear is "False Evidence Appearing Real." That is, we choose to believe what we see over what God has said. Fear causes us to stop, turn back, or even ignore what God has called us to do. We allow our limitations and those others put on us to keep us in a box.

Well, we don't serve a God Who wants us in a box! The Spirit of God commands us to walk in the power of God. It leads us to walk with the love of God. And it encourages us to live with God's discipline. Whatever God calls us to, He has already provided the pathway to do it.

We are imbued with His power, covered by His love, and walk in His authority (which keeps us subject to Him)! We fight from victory! Let's stop believing the false evidence and walk in the victory already won for us through our Lord and Savior, Jesus Christ.

#ArmorUp!!

A New Commandment:
Love One Another

Good morning, brothers!

"So now I am giving you a new commandment: Love each other. Just as I have loved you, you should love each other. Your love for one another will prove to the world that you are My disciples" (John 13:34-35).

The love we show for others is a reflection of the Lord. How can we claim to be Christians or Christ-like if we don't love as He would? The world loves us for what we can do for them. Jesus loves us to death. He put His life up for our benefit. Can we put the best interest of the Lord (and others) before our own?

In a world that tells us to do what is best for us and to "live our truth," that is a difficult stance to take. We are constantly bombarded by examples of people putting themselves first and expecting others to sacrifice for them. Jesus' commandment seems foolish to this logic.

Just because we live in this world that doesn't love like Jesus doesn't mean we have to live by its rules. We need to step up and step out of the conventional wisdom of the day. Let's light a path to a better way of living. Let's walk as Jesus walked. Let's let love shine through. Let's show the world how life is supposed to be! Let's seek the best for others, not requiring anything in return. Now that's love!

#ArmorUp!!!

How to Love One Another

Good morning, brothers!

"Dear friends, since God loved us that much, we surely ought to love each other. No one has ever seen God. But if we love each other, God lives in us, and His love is brought to full expression in us" (1 John 4:11-12).

Love seeks the best good for someone else and expects nothing in return. God's love has no strings attached—it is unconditional. We tend to love only those who love or treat us the way we want to be treated.

Jesus showed compassion for all Jerusalem when He lamented over them in Matthew 23:37. He didn't pick and choose. Neither should we! Let's seek the best good for others today. When we care for others, we can be sure the Lord will take care of us!

#ArmorUp!!!

In Hot Pursuit

Good morning, brothers!

"Whoever pursues righteousness and unfailing love will find life, righteousness, and honor" (Proverbs 21:21).

Here's another simple promise in God's Word. Pursuing requires relentless chasing. One does not give up until he overtakes the thing he is pursuing. The world encourages us to join the rat race that pursues wealth, power, and happiness. Chasing those things leaves us empty, frustrated, and disappointed. They will never satisfy us. That race leads to a dead end.

We need to chase after righteousness and unfailing love. The Lord tells us what we should place value in and what we should chase after. Choosing righteousness and unfailing love lead to the most fulfilling of lives. While chasing these things, we are blessed with life, righteousness, and honor. In Him, we find satisfaction and the desire to keep going.

If we want to live a fulfilling and joyous life, let's get out of the rat race and run the race the Lord set before us. Let's leave the dead-end pursuit and pursue life everlasting! Never stop chasing, brothers!!!

#ArmorUp!!!

Beauty Is Only Skin Deep

Good morning, brothers!

"Charm is deceptive, and beauty does not last; but a woman who fears the LORD will be greatly praised" (Proverbs 31:30).

While the world defines beauty and charm as valuable and something worth pursuing, fearing the Lord is eternally valuable. Focus on seeking a woman who values serving the Lord above all else. Let's take time today to love, encourage, and celebrate the godly women in our lives.

Our mothers may not have been perfect, but God made them perfect for us! And He always makes up the difference where we fall short. A mother's love and support give her children wings to soar. She is the first member and president of our fan club. That's why every athlete who gets a camera in their face quickly waves and shouts, "Hi, Mom!"

Let's thank God for the mothers, both biological and otherwise who have nurtured, loved, cuddled, kissed, and even kicked us in those times we needed it. God bless the ladies He chose to give the gift to and especially those who accepted the responsibility with pride!

#ArmorUp!!!

Want to Control Your Mouth? Keep It Shut!

Good morning, brothers!

"Those who control their tongue will have a long life; opening your mouth can ruin everything" (Proverbs 13:3).

We read in Proverbs 18:21 that death and life are in the power of the tongue. We have to watch what we say and how we say it. Sometimes, even a well-intentioned comment can burn somebody else. Let's be mindful of the words we choose. Our choice of words should build others up and not tear them down.

Let's honor the Lord today with the words we speak and the words we don't speak! Sometimes the best thing we say is the thing we left unsaid!

#ArmorUp!!!

Don't Worry; Pray!

Good morning, brothers!

"Don't worry about anything; instead, pray about everything. Tell God what you need, and thank Him for all He has done" (Philippians 4:6).

Worry is the enemy of faith. Worry takes our focus from God. Peter walked on water at Jesus' command. Worry caused him to take his eyes off Jesus and focus on his surroundings instead. As a result, he began to sink. He doubted what Jesus told him to do.

Has God called us to do something? Won't He guide us through it? Where there is a vision, there is provision! We need to take our worries to the altar and leave them there. Has not God brought us this far? Hasn't He promised never to leave or forsake us? God has a proven track record. Thanking Him for what He has already done reminds us to continue to trust Him for what He will do.

Whatever we are doing or going through, we have to invite God in. The Lord is a gentleman. He will not go into a situation unless He is invited in (see Revelation 3:20). Although He already knows about it, He has yielded the authority to us. We need to ask Him to come in. However, once we invite Him in, we must allow Him to do what He does.

In other words, we need to surrender authority back to Him. Let's allow the Lord to drive today! And no backseat driving!

#ArmorUp!!!

Choose Love and Not Hate

Good morning, brothers!

"But to you who are willing to listen, I say, love your enemies! Do good to those who hate you. Bless those who curse you. Pray for those who hurt you" (Luke 6:27-28).

Wow! The Lord gives us no wiggle room here! Jesus leaves no stone unturned. The Lord challenges us to love even those who we find unlovable, even those we have a reason not to love. Love is unconditional. It's not a feeling; it's an action. It doesn't matter how we feel about them or how they may feel about us. I don't read where He says we have to like them or be their friends, but I do read we are to bless them, do good to them, and pray for them. Let's seek to be a blessing to everyone we come in contact with, regardless of how we feel about them.

We are to love others regardless of how they treat us! Forgiving them is not for their benefit, but for ours. It releases us from holding on to the anger and hatred and frees us to love as He loves. We have to let go of any negativity if we want to receive positivity. Love may cover a multitude of sins, but it washes away hate! Choose to love today!

#ArmorUp!!!

Trust God's Perfect Timing

Good morning, brothers!

"Whatever is good and perfect is a gift coming down to us from God our Father, who created all the lights in the heavens. He never changes or casts a shifting shadow" (James 1:17).

Light can create shadows, but it cannot cast a shadow. Not only did the Lord create light, but He is also the Light of the World! The Lord looks to shine His Light upon us daily.

Have you ever gotten a gift that was "just what you needed"? Have you ever been looking for something and found just what you were looking for? Have you ever gotten something that was just perfect for you, and you weren't even looking for it? Those are all blessings from God! Think about it. It could have been something as minor as a parking spot. It could be as major as a promotion at work or a clean bill of health. God is always looking out for us and looking for opportunities to bless us.

God doesn't give poor gifts! He knows just what we need, and His timing is perfect! We have to wait on Him! Just as a parent knows what to give a child and when to give it to them, the Lord knows what is best for us! We need to trust His timing and wait for His deliverance! The problem is we don't always recognize His gifts or acknowledge Him for the gifts.

Let's be on the lookout for God's goodness in our lives today, and thank Him when we see it!

#ArmorUp!!!

Facing Trials? Have No Fear!

Good morning, brothers!

"Don't be afraid, for I am with you. Don't be discouraged, for I am your God. I will strengthen you and help you. I will hold you up with my victorious right hand" (Isaiah 41:10).

Why do we get so down when we face trials? Things may look dim and gloomy, but we have the Champion of all champions on our side! The Lord God Almighty is with us!

When we align ourselves with Him and submit to His will, we will have great success! Don't look at the circumstances; look at the Savior, and watch what happens! He is always there to strengthen and hold us up. Because of the victory Jesus claimed at the cross, He can now lead us from victory. So, whatever we may face, we need to face it with the Lord. For when we face it with the Lord, we will be victorious! In this way, we fight from victory and not for victory. Trust Him!

#ArmorUp!!!

The Holy Spirit, Our Guide

Good morning, brothers

"So I say, let the Holy Spirit guide your lives. Then you won't be doing what your sinful nature craves" (Galatians 5:16).

When we relinquish the driver's seat, we give control to a new driver. We need to let that new driver be the Holy Spirit! When we follow the lead of the Spirit, He is only going to take us on the path that glorifies the Lord.

We won't have to worry about the sinful nature. The Holy Spirit has no relationship with the sinful nature of this world. Let's trust the Holy Spirit to guide us today and ride in victory!

#ArmorUp!!!

What Real Love Looks Like

Good morning, brothers!

"We know what real love is because Jesus gave up His life for us. So we also ought to give up our lives for our brothers and sisters" (1 John 3:16).

Remember, love seeks the best for someone else and does not expect anything in return. Jesus sacrificed His life to give us life. He endured the shame and pain of cross just so we could have a right relationship with God. He became our sin and example so that we could have a path back to God and know how to walk that path properly. There are no strings! The benefit is all ours!

Who are we willing to sacrifice anything for? The Lord's love has no limit or strings. Does ours? We have seen and experienced real love. Let's pass it on today!

#ArmorUp!!!

Ambassadors for Christ

Good morning, brothers!

"But you will receive power when the Holy Spirit comes upon you. And you will be my witnesses, telling people about me everywhere—in Jerusalem, throughout Judea, in Samaria, and to the ends of the earth" (Acts 1:8).

We are the only Bible some people will ever read. We are the Lord's ambassadors to the world. How well do we represent Him? No, we don't have to be perfect. We look to the Word to be perfected in us. We will stumble and even fall. However, we must not remain there, nor must we give up.

We must maintain our focus on the Lord and allow the Holy Spirit to guide us. We must repent and turn away from our sin and iniquities and get back on course. God has raised a standard in our lives. Let's represent it (and Him) well!

#ArmorUp!!!

Focus on Quality, Not Quantity

Good morning, brothers!

"As the Scriptures say, 'People are like grass; their beauty is like a flower in the field. The grass withers and the flower fades'" (1 Peter 1:24).

We know we are only temporary in this world. But, what do we do with the time we have? How much love do we share while we are here? What is our impact on those we touch? It's not how much time we have that matters as much as the impact we have on the lives we come into contact with. We need to focus on the quality and not the quantity of the days we are blessed with. Let's not be weeds that just grow for our own benefit and are good for nothing and thrown away. What we provide for others that will last. Let's make a difference with the time we have been given! Seek to be a blessing today!

#ArmorUp!!!

You Will Reap What You Sow

Good morning, brothers!

"Don't be misled—you cannot mock the justice of God. You will always harvest what you plant. Those who live only to satisfy their own sinful nature will harvest decay and death from that sinful nature. But those who live to please the Spirit will harvest everlasting life from the Spirit" (Galatians 6:7-8).

What goes around comes around. There are consequences for our actions. God gave us the freedom to choose our actions, but we can't choose the consequences of those actions. We try to operate outside of God's will and expect Him to bless us. It doesn't work like that.

We have to make sure our actions and our motives are true. Let's be mindful of what we put into the world today. Our negative thoughts yield negative results. Our positive thoughts yield positive results. It's that simple. If we choose to live a life away from the Lord, we open ourselves up to consequences outside of God's will. We can cry and ask, "Where is God?" and "why doesn't He love me?" as much as we want.

God loves us enough to give us our freedom. It is we who don't love Him enough to obey and follow Him! We want God's blessings without His commandments. Like the commercial says, "that's not how it works, that's not how any of this works." When we plant submission and obedience, we get God's blessings. When we seek to be a blessing, we are blessed. God will honor that which honors Him! Let's plant wisely!

#ArmorUp!!!

Who Do You Look Like?

Good morning, brothers!

"For the grace of God has been revealed, bringing salvation to all people. And we are instructed to turn from godless living and sinful pleasures. We should live in this evil world with wisdom, righteousness, and devotion to God" (Titus 2:11-12).

God's grace has allowed us to become the children of God! As His children, we should live a life that reflects who He is. Some people who know my parents will say I look, act, or say things that remind them of one of my parents. I always say that should be true because I am a product of both of them.

Shouldn't it be the same way with God? Shouldn't people say we've said or done something that reminds them of the Lord? Are we truly a reflection of the One by whose name we call ourselves?

#ArmorUp!!!

We Are Victorious!

Good morning, brothers!

"What shall we say about such wonderful things as these? If God is for us, who can ever be against us?" (Romans 8:31).

Have any of you watched or attended a Harlem Globetrotters game? All the showmanship is great. It's very entertaining. But the thing I notice the most is they always win! The Washington Generals put forth their best effort, but always come up short. They may be ahead for a quarter or two, but they always lose.

Our daily walk should be the same way! The devil will do his best to thwart our progress. He may even be ahead at some point, but we will ALWAYS win!!! We have the Lord God Almighty on our side!

When Jesus said in John 19:30, "It is finished," that secured our victory! We have to walk in faith to our victory. We fight the fight of faith from victory! Let's remember whose team we're on today! Walk in victory!!!

#ArmorUp!!!

The Heart of the Matter

Good morning, brothers!

"Create in me a clean heart, O God. Renew a loyal spirit within me" (Psalm 51:10).

Have you ever tried to fix something and only made it worse by your attempt? David was wallowing in sin, and his attempts to cover it only made things worse. He was now broken and dejected. However, he knew there was one place he could go to be fixed.

He went to the Lord—back to his Creator. David was known as a man after God's own heart. Reading his penitent prayer in Psalm 51 is a great example of why. He recognized the blame for his sin fell squarely on himself, and he accepted the responsibility for it. He also knew he couldn't find his way back to the right place with the Lord. He presented himself before the Lord. He humbly asked to be cleansed.

We all have made choices that take us deeper into the darkness and further away from our true destiny. The Cathedrals, in their song, "Sin Will Take You Farther" sing, "sin will take you farther than you want to go, keep you longer than you want to stay and cost you more than you are willing to pay." The only way back is to turn to the Lord. Jesus has already paid the price for our sins—past, present, and future. We have to be willing to turn to Him and follow Him.

Our loving Lord is waiting with open arms to take us back. But, are we willing to leave our sin behind? Are we willing to forgive ourselves for our past mistakes? Do we have the faith to move forward with the clean slate we have been given by Christ? Jesus gives us a clean heart when we come to Him.

#ArmorUp!!!

Use the GPS

Good morning, brothers!

"Praise the Lord; praise God our Savior! For each day He carries us in His arms" (Psalm 68:19).

The Lord is there. Even when we think we are "doing it ourselves!" We don't realize that His hands are redirecting things so that they work for our good. We only think about the pain, frustration and setbacks. God is like a GPS. He knows our destination and all the problems and situations ahead of us. When we listen to Him, He will give us along the best and safest (but not necessarily the quickest) route to our destination. Funny how we have more confidence in the **G**lobal **P**ositioning **S**ystem (**GPS**) and are more willing to trust and follow it than **G**od's **P**lan for our **S**alvation!

Thank you, Lord for Your willingness to guide us! We need to realize that no matter what we are going through that God is present. We just need to invite Him in. But, when He comes in, it is to take control. We need to be willing to relinquish control! We are victorious in Him! He will lead us safely to where we need to be. Which GPS are we going to put our trust in today? Recalculating...

#ArmorUp!!!

You Must Surrender to Win!

Good morning, brothers!

"So humble yourselves before God. Resist the devil, and he will flee from you" (James 4:7).

Resistance is futile. Those are the words the hero would hear from his enemy in TV shows and movies. Our enemy tells us the same thing through experiences and even friends and family. They are right. In our strength, resistance is futile. We can't resist a spiritual enemy for long using natural strength. We have to acknowledge that, in and of ourselves, we can't have the victory over the devil. We can't live a God-fearing life by ourselves. We must come to the Lord and surrender to His authority. Once we are under His covering, then we have the power to resist and overcome any attack of the enemy. It's not by our might or our power.

James tells us there is something we must do first. We have to tap into the Lord's strength. How do we do that? We must humble ourselves before God. We must acknowledge Him. We must realize we need His guidance and submit to His will. No enemy is too great or powerful when facing the Almighty! We must be under the Lord's covering to resist.

When we rely on our strength, we will succumb to the enemy's attacks. When we surrender to the Lord, we will overcome the attacks and snares of the enemy. We will yield to someone. Why not choose to yield to the Victorious One? Submit to the Lord today!

#ArmorUp!!!

Living Before Others

Good morning, brothers!

"Live wisely among those who are not believers, and make the most of every opportunity. Let your conversation be gracious and attractive so that you will have the right response for everyone" (Colossians 4:5-6).

We understand we are the only Bible some people will ever read. Therefore, our lives are the only representation of the Lord some people will pay attention to. That doesn't mean we have to live perfectly before others. We should live honestly before them. We have the same struggles and strifes as they do. Being a Christian makes us no different from them. They just need to see how we respond to those struggles and strifes and overcome them through Jesus! We are not better, just blessed! Draw others to the Lord by your righteous living.

#ArmorUp!!!

Fear the Lord

Good morning, brothers!

"Fear of the LORD is the foundation of wisdom. Knowledge of the Holy One results in good judgment" (Proverbs 9:10).

The fear of the Lord here is taking God seriously and being willing to submit to His authority. As we get to know God, we think and act as He does. Have you ever noticed how the more time you spend with someone, the more you two say the same things? Something similar happens when we spend time with God. He rubs off on us, but we don't rub off on Him. Spending time with Him allows us to get to know Him and gain the wisdom to think and act as He does.

God is the Source of wisdom. James says anyone who desires wisdom should ask the Lord (James 1:5). Our fear of the Lord, that respect for His power and authority that causes us to obey Him, is the foundation of our wisdom. We would be wise to submit to the Lord and obey His will for our lives.

When we begin getting to know the Lord for ourselves by studying His Word and praying, we learn of His ways. Our relationship with Him enables us to obtain wisdom. Our knowledge of Him plus our application of His ways is wisdom. Make an effort to walk with the Lord today!

#ArmorUp!!!

True Worship

Good morning, brothers!

"And so, dear brothers and sisters, I plead with you to give your bodies to God because of all He has done for you. Let them be a living and holy sacrifice—the kind He will find acceptable. This is truly the way to worship Him" (Romans 12:1).

The apostle Paul tells us our best act of worship to God is to surrender our bodies to the Lord. That means we follow God's plan for our lives and yield to His will even when our minds tell us to do something else. We are strong-willed individuals. Many times, when God's will contradicts our own, we try to find a compromise. We try to sacrifice something else instead. Samuel told King Saul, "Obedience is better than sacrifice" (1 Samuel 15:22).

God is not Monty Hall or Wayne Brady, and we are not playing *Let's Make a Deal!* If we want to follow the Lord, then we have to be all in. There are no shortcuts or compromises that will take the place of true obedience. Let's stop playing games with God and get it together!

#ArmorUp!!!

In the World and Not of It

Good morning, brothers!

"Don't copy the behavior and customs of this world, but let God transform you into a new person by changing the way you think. Then you will learn to know God's will for you, which is good and pleasing and perfect" (Romans 12:2).

How can we repay God for all He has done for us? We can't! And, He doesn't want us to! We can, however, show our gratitude by living a life that pleases Him. St. Ambrose, the bishop of Milan (387 AD), coined the phrase, "when in Rome do as the Romans do."

Paul persuades us to do the opposite. We should stand out or rather be outstanding in our thoughts and deeds. We should be representatives of the Most High. We need to think and act as He would. Just because something is popular doesn't make it right. Many times, the right thing won't be the popular thing. Choose right over popular and watch God move on your behalf. Stay on His course and ...

#ArmorUp!!!

Get Wisdom

Good morning, brothers!

"Getting wisdom is the wisest thing you can do! And whatever else you do, develop good judgment" (Proverbs 4:7).

Wisdom is knowledge we gain from experience. For example, someone is told don't touch an iron because it's hot and they don't touch it. That person has knowledge about the iron. The person who has been burned by an iron before knows it is wise not to touch it.

Good judgment is when we apply the wisdom we have obtained. We know that just because we know better, we don't always do better! All of us have touched that iron of sin even though we know it burns!

God has blessed us with wisdom and knowledge. It is up to us to apply them daily. That is why Solomon says to develop good judgment. We must put wisdom into practice. We've got the game plan. Let's put it into practice and ...

#ArmorUp!!!

Enduring Temptation

Good morning, brothers!

"God blesses those who patiently endure testing and temptation. Afterward they will receive the crown of life that God has promised to those who love Him" (James 1:12).

We all will be tested and tempted. God has equipped us with the ability to endure testing and avoid temptation. We must develop that endurance. We don't have to have test anxiety! It is an OPEN BOOK TEST!

The Holy Spirit is with us to guide us in all truth. So whatever we face today, we have help to overcome it. We need to study the Word and believe in the Teacher. We must use what the Lord has given us (the previous experiences of both ourselves and others, along with the Bible).to help us overcome!

We may have stumbled and even fallen, but the Lord can deliver us still if we are willing to turn to Him and surrender. We are never too far gone! God can bring us through any situation and circumstance we are facing. We must look to the Lord and trust Him in every situation we face. He is faithful and will deliver us if we trust and follow Him. He will give us peace in the midst of it all and a crown at the end. Let's walk in the victory of Christ today!

#ArmorUp!!!

Beware the Favor of Man

Good morning, brothers!

"[T]ook palm branches and went down the road to meet Him. They shouted, 'Praise God! Blessings on the one who comes in the name of the Lord! Hail to the King of Israel'" (John 12:13).

Be careful seeking man's approval! The world seeks to put you on a pedestal only to shoot you down. One day they were singing Jesus' praises, and less than a week later, they were shouting, "Crucify Him!" The whole time His focus was on doing the will of the Father.

We should not seek fame and fortune or the approval of men. They are fleeting. God's favor and approval are sufficient if you stay focused on Him. You'll find peace in that journey, and the reward is everlasting!!!

#ArmorUp!!!

God Always Had a Plan

Good morning, brothers!

"But He was pierced for our rebellion, crushed for our sins. He was beaten so we could be whole. He was whipped so we could be healed" (Isaiah 53:5).

The God of creation had a plan for when we messed up. He would come down Himself in the form of the Son and be the perfect sacrifice that would allow His creation a way back to Him! He put Himself in the game so that we would win!

I remember playing football video games and creating a player so dominant that he took over any game when he had the ball. Well, God did the same thing! The Creator of the Game put a dominant Player in the game of life, but He played the game by the rules the Creator designed for the game, not by the way we THINK the game should be played.

The world and the enemy thought He (and we) lost by the sacrifice. Oh, but no! We are victorious! The Master of the game created a Masterpiece that gave us a certain victory! Hallelujah!!! Hosanna in the Highest! Blessed is He who comes in the name of the Lord!

#ArmorUp!!!

He Is Alive!!!

Good morning, brothers!

"He isn't here! He is risen from the dead, just as He said would happen. Come, see where His body was lying" (Matthew 28:6).

Hallelujah!!! He has risen, and we along with Him! God's redemption plan is complete, and we are the beneficiaries! We need to live as though we serve a risen Savior and not as defeated followers.

If we believe He is who He says He is and did what the Word says He did, then why are we so down? Face the challenges of life head-on and know this risen Savior has overcome all obstacles we may face. He did it so that we could do it as well. Rejoice today as we commemorate His victory, but we must go out and claim our own! Victory is ours!

#ArmorUp!!!

Study the Word

Good morning, brothers!

"Study this Book of Instruction continually. Meditate on it day and night so you will be sure to obey everything written in it. Only then will you prosper and succeed in all you do" (Joshua 1:8).

When we purchase something new, it comes with an owner's manual. If we want to use our new purchase properly, we read the owner's manual. It provides us with all the information we need to successfully operate our new toy.

The Bible is our owner's manual. God has provided us with the **B**asic **I**nstructions **B**efore **L**eaving **E**arth (BIBLE)! Jesus is our living example of the Word of God. We need to follow in His footsteps and obey the Father's precepts to have His success. The Bible is not a good luck charm to travel with or a magic lamp to rub and get wishes granted. In the Bible, we find the keys to living as God desires. We need to open it and read it. Like Agnes Allen said, "when all else fails, read the instructions!"

#ArmorUp!!!

New Day, New Mercies

Good morning, brothers!

"The faithful love of the Lord never ends! His mercies never cease. Great is His faithfulness; His mercies begin afresh each morning" (Lamentations 3:22-23).

Oh! How merciful and faithful is the Lord! He is always aware of us and our situations. When looking back over our lives, we can see the hand of God throughout. We know He is faithful because we see where He has shown up both in our lives and the lives of others. We know He is merciful because we have been blessed with many things we don't deserve. Each new day is proof of His mercy.

Romans 6:23 says, "The wages of sin is death." We know we sin, and we aren't dead yet! So, there's still hope. We must turn away from our sinful desires and turn to Christ. He died so that we could be free from sin—not free to sin.

New day, new mercies! We need to approach each day with this mindset. God gives us another opportunity to learn of Him and provides us with just what we need to make it through today. Our problem is we are still focusing on yesterday, last week, or too busy worrying about tomorrow or next week. Trust in God's faithfulness and accomplish the tasks set before you today. Surrender to the Lord. Allow Him to lead you today!

#ArmorUp!!!

What Is Most Valuable? (Part 1)

Good morning, brothers!

"Don't love money; be satisfied with what you have. For God has said, 'I will never fail you. I will never abandon you'" (Hebrews 13:5).

We have been duped into believing that, like Malcolm Forbes said, "He who dies with the most toys, wins!" The pursuit of things or riches should not be our purpose. That doesn't mean we are not to desire being successful. But if our focus is in the glory of the things we gain, we have lost sight of what is most important. What becomes important to us when we pursue things is the next thing. We will never be satisfied with things!

We should seek to bring glory to God in all we do. Our relationship with Him should be first. Seeking to be a blessing to others should be next. Then we should look after ourselves. There is security in knowing God won't fail or abandon us. He will ensure we have what we need in whatever situation we are going through. We need to focus on serving Him wherever we are and trust Him to make up the difference to get us to where we need to be!

#ArmorUp!!!

What Is Most Valuable? (Part 2)

Good morning, brothers!

"Do not love this world nor the things it offers you, for when you love the world, you do not have the love of the Father in you. For the world offers only a craving for physical pleasure, a craving for everything we see, and pride in our achievements and possessions. These are not from the Father, but are from this world" (1 John 2:15-16).

The world tries to convince us the pursuit of pleasure, possessions, and positions is the pathway to success. Everything we do in the world revolves around these three motivators. When we dig deeper into some life decisions we've made, we can see one or more of these three at the root.

Jesus says in Matthew 6:33 to seek God's kingdom and righteousness first. John tells us here to love the Lord instead of loving the world or its things. God wants to bless us. However, He just doesn't want us to focus on the blessings. When we focus on the gifts more than the Giver, we are losing sight of our purpose and run afoul of God's plan for our lives.

Are we using God as a genie? Are we serving Him to get whatever blessings we can out of Him? Or, are we focused on Him and desiring to be a blessing to both Him and others? Where is our allegiance? The trinity of the world (pleasure, possessions, and positions).or the Holy Trinity (Father, Son, and Holy Spirit)?

#ArmorUp!!!

Heart Examination (Part 1)

Good morning, brothers!

"But I, the LORD, search all hearts and examine secret motives. I give all people their due rewards, according to what their actions deserve" (Jeremiah 17:10).

We all have hopes, dreams, and fantasies. Many of them we are willing to share, but we keep some hidden from everyone. The Lord also has a plan for our lives, and He is checking to see if our motives will line up with His plan for us. He wants to reward those hidden desires that will truly benefit us, so He examines our hearts and creates a plan to get us there.

When we have a relationship with God, our mindset changes. Old thoughts may arise, but we have to put them to death and follow the Lord. We can achieve our desires with our plan, but God won't be anywhere in it. God won't honor what doesn't honor Him! God's plan for us is better than any fantasy we could create for ourselves! God's plan for us will help us achieve our innermost dreams and beyond and will have guaranteed success. We just have to trust Him and stay on His path.

We may not get to those places when we thought we would, but the Lord will give us the desires of our hearts in due time. We need to trust the Author of the Universe and seek His plan for our lives. We won't be disappointed!

#ArmorUp!!!

Heart Examination (Part 2)

Good morning, brothers!

"People may be right in their own eyes, but the LORD examines their heart" (Proverbs 21:2).

The world is constantly telling people to "live in their truth." The world defines truth as what it accepts as truth. By that definition, truth could be whatever we feel or want it to be. We see that unfolding all around us.

That would make truth relative or based on emotions. Truth is not relative. Truth is what God says about a thing and is absolute. Truth doesn't change from one person to the next. Jesus says in John 14:6, "I am, the Way, the Truth and the Life." If He is the same yesterday, today, and forever, how can we say truth changes?

It doesn't matter what we think about our actions. We must align ourselves with God's plan. Get your mind right, and get your heart right! The world tells us it's ok to "walk in your truth." If your truth is not aligned with the Truth, then it's a lie. Your truth has been confused with reality.

Reality changes. Truth NEVER changes! Water is still water, whether it's a solid (ice), liquid, or gas (water vapor). Its state may have changed (reality), but it's truth (water) has not. Make sure you focus more on living in truth than in your reality. Let's make sure we do it for the right reason-to glorify God!

#ArmorUp!!!

48

DAY

There's Safety in Numbers

Good morning, brothers!

"For where two or three gather together as my followers, I am there among them" (Matthew 18:20).

Let's face it; going it alone is tough. I admire self-starters. It has always been difficult for me to exercise, clean up, or start most projects by myself. But when I have a partner, I seem to get really motivated. The Lord understands my pain! He endorses group work! As few as two people is all He needs. We don't need to go it alone. What a comfort to know that when we gather together to serve the Lord, He is there with us! Two like-minded individuals and Jesus is all we need! When Jesus is involved, there is a majority!

Don't isolate yourself on this journey. God never meant for you to do it on your own. Find God-loving, God-fearing, and God-obeying people to walk with you—even if it's just one. The two of you and God make a majority. Follow the Lord's pathway together. Walk in victory together with Christ! Praise God for His promise!

#ArmorUp!!!

Controlled by Love

Good morning, brothers!

"Either way, Christ's love controls us. Since we believe that Christ died for all, we also believe that we have all died to our old life. He died for everyone so that those who receive his new life will no longer live for themselves. Instead, they will live for Christ, who died and was raised for them" (2 Corinthians 5:14-15).

If Christ made the ultimate sacrifice for us, then why can't we surrender to Him? When we do give our lives to Him, then we can live a new life. We are no longer obligated to do things because "that's the way I am." We are free to choose how we live.

The bondage of sin is no more! We who accept Christ are free to live as He lived, totally trusting in the Father and not according to the world's standard. Let's live the new, free life God gave us today!

#ArmorUp!!!

The Key to Success

Good morning, brothers!

"Commit your actions to the LORD, and your plans will succeed" (Proverbs 16:3).

In other words, when we align ourselves with God, we have guaranteed success! We can't continue to do it our way and only reach out to the Lord when we want Him to bail us out of trouble. God will authorize those things that align with His will.

How do we get to know His will? When we choose to spend time with the Lord and study His Word, we think and act as He does. Our actions align with His desires. We begin to walk in victory. Success will follow.

Do you believe God? Do you believe He is Who He says He is and will do what He says He will do? If so, then commit your ways to Him. Align yourself with the Almighty and watch as success overtakes you like a flood! God knows where you've been, where you are, and where you are going. The question is, will you go where He wants to take you? Align yourself with the Victorious One! God honors those who honor Him!

#ArmorUp!!!

No Shortcuts to Success

Good morning, brothers!

"Joyful are those who obey His laws and search for Him with all their hearts" (Psalm 119:2).

When we set our focus on the Lord and follow His commands, we will find joy and peace. The sailing will not always be smooth, but, with the Lord, it will be bearable. We have to avoid all the distractions and "shortcuts" we find or create that keep us from staying on His path. The Cathedrals song, "Sin Will Take You Farther" reminds us that "sin will take you farther than you want to go, keep you longer than you want to stay, and cost you more than you want to pay!" So much for being a shortcut! Let's stay on track today. Father, we ask for Your grace to keep us away from the distractions that so easily draw our attention away from our focus on You. May we find the joy that comes from following You today. In Jesus' name, Amen!

Many people try to encourage us by saying there will be joy at the end of the journey. That sometimes is discouraging when we're in the midst of a storm. We want to have hope for the present, not just for the future. The psalmist says, "joyful are those" That means there is joy on the journey! Let's follow the Lord's plan and obey His commands. God will be with us every step of the way, and there will be rejoicing at the end of our journey!

#ArmorUp!!!

If You Get Angry, Don't Stay Angry

Good morning, brothers!

"And 'don't sin by letting anger control you.' Don't let the sun go down while you are still angry, for anger give a foothold to the devil" (Ephesians 4:26-27).

Anger is an emotion that requires gratification. It must be fed to be satisfied. Once it's fed, it seems to go dormant again, but it only grows bigger and hungrier the next time it awakens. Sin seems to be its food of choice. Retaliation and retribution are its favorite dishes. The longer it stays around, the more it seems to control us. According to this Scripture, anger is one way the devil can sneak into our lives.

We have to put our anger under subjection. We have to control it. We cannot let it fester and grow out of control. Like a gremlin, we can't "feed it after midnight." We can't sleep on our anger. The longer it hangs around, the more it tries to take over. Anger tends to lead us away from the will of God and opens the door for the devil to walk in. The Lord has told us that vengeance is His responsibility. Anger tells us that we need to seek our own revenge. We can't let anger take the wheel.

If we let our anger fester, those negative ideas begin to dance around in our heads and distract us from God's purpose for our lives. We just have to deal with it spiritually.

#ArmorUp!!!

God Is Faithful

Good morning, brothers!

"Let us hold tightly without wavering to the hope we affirm, for God can be trusted to keep His promise" (Hebrews 10:23).

When we walk the path with the Lord, we can rest assured that success is in its way. It doesn't matter how it looks or feels. God sees the past, present, and future all at the same time. We have to trust His plan and not get distracted by our interpretations (or misinterpretations).

God's will is perfect. When we are in His will, it will directly lead where He desires us to be. We have to rest in that fact. There will be distractions and people trying to lure us away, but we have to trust the process and stay in God's will. God promises to never leave us, and He always keeps His promises. Stay the course, and watch what happens!

#ArmorUp!!!

Don't Go It Alone

Good morning, brothers!

"Share each other's burdens, and in this way obey the law of Christ" (Galatians 6:2).

We are stronger together. Two people carrying a load is easier than one. Two people carrying two loads are also easier than each of us carrying our own. On this Christian journey, we need to help each other make it through. Pitfalls and traps are everywhere. It's hard to recognize them if we are too focused on the things we are carrying.

Help a brother out! Accept help from a brother! We don't have to go it alone. Don't let someone you know go it alone. We have to be strong enough to admit when we need help.

Don't reject the blessing God sends to help you! Trust the Lord to send the right people to help you. Listen to the Lord when He sends you to help others. The journey is sweeter when you have people to share it with. We need to share our experiences to help each other navigate the challenges we face.

My pastor, Carl E. Jones, Sr. says, "**been through** is the only person who can tell **going through** how to **get through**." The enemy wants us to believe we are the only man who is experiencing or has experienced this. The book of Revelation tells us the believers overcame by the blood of the Lamb and their testimony (12:11). We need to continue sharing, encouraging, and praying. Victory is ours!!!

#ArmorUp!!!

The Lord Is a Fortress

Good morning, brothers!

"The name of the LORD is a strong fortress; the godly run to Him and are safe" (Proverbs 18:10).

The Lord is not just a Fortress, but a strong Fortress! He has been tested and tried and proven to ALWAYS be reliable. Whatever we are going through, we need to take it to the Lord. We need to allow Him to be our Protector and our Champion. No enemy can triumph over Him! He has never lost a battle! Victory is secure! Go to Him and be safe!

Safety and peace are in the Lord's hands. We will face storms in life. Being in the Lord guarantees us passage through those storms. Even if situations don't turn out the way we expect, it doesn't mean we have lost. Paul tells us in Romans 8:28, "God causes all things work together for the good." We love to quote that part of the verse, but we tend to miss the rest of it: "to those that love God and are called according to His purpose for them." In other words, we have to love the Lord enough to align ourselves with Him and obey His will. We have to seek God's purpose for our lives. In Him, we find peace, protection, and purpose.

#ArmorUp!!!

Go All In

Good morning, brothers!

"And you must love the LORD your God with all your heart, all your soul, and all your strength" (Deuteronomy 6:5).

We want the Lord to be all in for us but aren't all in with Him. The Lord is waiting for us to commit to Him fully. He is faithful to do all He has promised us, but He wants a commitment from us first. How can we say we love the Lord when we are halfhearted? He wasn't halfhearted in His sacrifice. Did He sacrifice **all** so that we could give just **some**?

We want to "see and then believe." Well, the Lord challenges us to believe and then see. He calls us to act and see—not wait and see. Love is not a passive stance. It is an active approach. We must show the Lord we love Him by putting our faith into action. He doesn't say love the Lord with all your sight!

Let's commit ourselves fully to the Lord and watch the results. He is worth our time and effort! Let's not meet Him halfway. Let's go all in today! The Lord withholds nothing from us, so let's not withhold anything from Him. We must love the Lord with all your heart, soul, strength, and ...

#ArmorUp!!!

Know When to Keep Quiet

Good morning, brothers!

"Even fools are thought wise when they keep silent; with their mouths shut, they seem intelligent" (Proverbs 17:28).

Have you ever been in a meeting and felt like you just had to say something to feel like you were a part of that meeting? Then you say the most random off-topic thing, and everybody looks at you like, "what are you talking about?" I've been that guy before, and it's embarrassing!

We have to learn that every one of our thoughts does not have to come out. We don't have to share all our opinions. Sometimes our presence alone is enough to bring to the table. Sometimes a simple "amen" or "I agree" will do. Now, before commenting, I ask myself the following: 1. Is it relevant? 2. How does my comment add value? 3. Is it necessary? 4. Does it glorify God?

Sometimes I ignore this wise counsel and fall flat, but I keep trying. Don't give up on the self-examinations. Keep growing, and ...

#ArmorUp!!!

Do Good and Share

Good morning, brothers!

"And don't forget to do good and to share with those in need. These are the sacrifices that please God" (Hebrews 13:16).

This is a simple truth. It is concise, clear, and easy to understand. Here are the sacrifices that please God—do good and share with those in need. Sometimes, we have our own idea of what service to the Lord looks like. We want to serve the Lord on our terms and expect Him to bless us because of our sacrifices for Him.

Just because we give up something "in the name of the Lord" doesn't mean it is pleasing to the Lord—especially when we take pride in the sacrifices. The Lord wants us to look outside ourselves. Pleasing God is not about satisfying our needs, but meeting the needs of others. The good we do should benefit others and draw them to the Lord. When our focus leaves us and shifts to pleasing God by helping others, we learn to trust that God looks out for us and our needs. That's when we are all blessed!

Today, let's do good and serve others. Not for what it will do for us, but just because it will bless them. That is pleasing to God.

#ArmorUp!!!

Trust in the Lord

Good morning, brothers!

"Trust in the LORD with all your heart; do not depend on your own understanding. Seek His will in all you do, and He will show you which path to take" (Proverbs 3:5-6).

Here is one of the Lord's simple commands with a promise tied to it. When we do our part, the Lord will most certainly do His part! We say people with heart are strong-willed and determined. God is telling us when we are fully determined to trust and seek Him in every circumstance, then He will always guide us the right way.

We need to involve the Lord in everything we do today and watch Him guide us through. Acknowledging His presence in everything is the key. He cares about every detail of our lives. We need to invite Him in and trust His wisdom to lead us. Trust in the Lord today and ...

#ArmorUp!!!

Who Is Your Source?

Good morning, brothers!

"Jesus told her, 'I am the Resurrection and the Life. Anyone who believes in Me will live, even after dying. Everyone who lives in Me and believes in Me will never ever die. Do you believe this, Martha?'" (John 11:25-26).

Death thought it had another captive in Jesus, but it was wrong! Jesus reclaimed for us the power over death. Now our physical death doesn't have to lead to spiritual death as well. In Jesus, we have been given the blessing of eternal life. That is, we no longer have to be separated from God. His death, burial, and resurrection have provided the pathway back to a right relationship with God. We have to believe in Jesus and follow His example to experience life eternal.

Do we trust Jesus as our source? No matter what happens, God has a plan for us. He is working it for our good, even when it doesn't look or feel good. Our triumphs are won by going through trials. Look to Jesus through them and watch what happens! If we truly serve the Lord, the only thing that is final is eternity with Him!

We all have the right to choose our path. However, following Jesus' path is the only way to have eternal life. All other paths lead to certain death. Let's examine ourselves and choose the path that leads to life! Let's believe in Him and ...

#ArmorUp!!!

Jesus Has Been There and Done That

Good morning, brothers!

"'I am the Alpha and the Omega—the Beginning and the End,' says the Lord God. 'I am the One who is, who always was, and who is still to come—the Almighty One'" (Revelation 1:8).

Just in case we were still wondering, Jesus lets us know who He really is! He's been here from start to finish! It all begins and ends with Him! We like to use the excuse that nobody knows our story. No one has walked our path. Not so! Jesus has been with us every step of the way.

Nothing is new to Him, and nothing will come as a surprise to Him. We have to listen to His directions as we walk the path He has for us. Submit your will to the Lord today and...

#ArmorUp!!!

There Is Life in Obedience

Good morning, brothers!

"I will never forget your commandments, for by them You give me life" (Psalm 119:93).

There are consequences tied to both obedience and disobedience. David tells the Lord he understands this truth and chooses to remember what God has told Him because there is life in obedience. We try to muddy the waters when it comes to serving God. We think it has to be more complicated than that, but it's not!

Choose to serve the Lord and obey His commands and see life. Don't follow, and death is certain. Let's choose wisely today and...

#ArmorUp!!!

Live in Peace

Good morning, brothers!

"And let the peace that comes from Christ rule in your hearts. For as members of one body you are called to live in peace. And always be thankful" (Colossians 3:15).

Living in peace with others doesn't mean we agree on everything. After all, we all have different perspectives, personalities, and experiences. However, as believers, we do have one thing in common. We are all children of Christ and must agree to operate to glorify Him. We all have different assignments to accomplish the one task of glorifying God. How we interact with one another is a key indicator of the love of Christ.

Coexisting and co-laboring can be difficult. But, when we allow the peace of the Lord to dwell in us, it becomes easier than we could ever have imagined. We have to trust the Lord to make up the difference in us and our relationships with others.

No matter what is going on around us, those of us in Christ have His peace inside. The question is do we let it rule in our hearts? Do we focus on the turmoil without or the peace within? We know God has a plan for us, but do we rest in that truth or worry? Thank God for the challenges we face! It steers us where He wants us to go and proves our need for Him daily. Let's live in peace today and ...

#ArmorUp!!!

Keep Moving Forward

Good morning, brothers!

"When doubts filled my mind, Your comfort gave me renewed hope and cheer" (Psalm 94:19).

How do we handle doubt? Where do we turn when doubts fill our minds? David knew not to listen to the doubts in his mind. He knew he needed to turn to His God for help. His confidence wasn't in himself.

When doubts come to thwart our progress and growth, we need to turn to the Lord. We need to turn to the Word for help. Family, friends, and loved ones are good, but they will fail us. The Lord never will! Call on Him in times of doubt. Trust that He will answer.

Doubts are like speed bumps. They may slow us down, but they shouldn't deter us from moving forward. When we doubt, we have to go back to our purpose for reassurance. Seek out the Lord and let His Word comfort you and keep you on the right path. We may question where we are and why we are there.

Are we doing what God called us to do? We need to stay the course until He directs us elsewhere. Trust the Lord and stay on His path. Allow the Holy Spirit to guide you. We have to keep moving forward and claim the victory that has been promised to those of us who believe. When in doubt, let's look to the Lord!

#ArmorUp!!!

Pay It Forward; Don't Payback

Good morning, brothers!

"See that no one pays back evil for evil, but always try to do good to each other and to all people" (1 Thessalonians 5:15).

Will Bowen says "hurt people hurt people." Many times, we seek to treat others the way they have treated us. We want those who have wronged us to feel what we have felt or are feeling. Paul challenges the believers at Thessalonica (and us).to change that behavior.

If we want to make a positive impact in our world, then we are to seek to love and do good to others regardless of how they treat us. We see and hear all the negative rhetoric being spewed by many world leaders and their followers. Then, their opponents choose to fight fire with fire in retaliation.

Revenge is not our responsibility. Vengeance belongs to the Lord. We are to treat others like we want them to treat us. Does it honor the Lord to cause someone else harm as payback?

Let's learn to forgive others as we want the Lord to forgive us. For, if He treated us like we treat others... I don't want to even think about that! Forgiveness is not for the other person. It frees us of a burden we weren't meant to bear. Let's stop trying to pay evil for evil. Let the Lord take care of the payback and pay the love forward.

#ArmorUp!!!

Slow on the Trigger

Good morning, brothers!

"Understand this, my dear brothers and sisters: You must all be quick to listen, slow to speak, and slow to get angry" (James 1:19).

In this fast-paced world we live in, we have been conditioned to move faster. I like to call it a "microwave society." We want everything as fast as possible, if not faster. In this Scripture passage, James is telling us to slow down when it comes to dealing with one another. We do need to be quick to listen, which is trying to understand the other party's perspective. Many times, we listen to respond and not to understand. Understanding doesn't mean we have to agree.

We need to be slow to speak. Allow time for understanding and then process a response based on that analysis and not just our "knee-jerk" reaction. That will help us be slow to get angry.

We can't allow our emotions to control us. We need to feel what we feel, but still deal with things the right way and not just do what makes us feel good. James doesn't say to ignore or suppress our emotions. We need to acknowledge them and deal with them appropriately. We need to take time to process them and respond in a manner that is right for the situation.

Let's focus on increasing our listening skills and decreasing our speech and taking time to process our emotions. That will improve our relationships.

#ArmorUp!!!

There Is None Like the Lord

Good morning, brothers!

"How great You are, O Sovereign LORD! There is no one like You. We have never even heard of another God like You!" (2 Samuel 7:22).

We try to put many things in the place of God, but nothing compares to Him! Nothing can soothe our pains, calm our fears, or give us the joy our God does. Everything we try to put in His place is terminal, meaning it has an end. Our God is everlasting, and He never fails! He is the Sovereign One. He not only rules, He super rules! He is in control of every situation. Nothing happens in our lives without His permission.

Some people ask why God allows bad things to happen. He allows us all to see the consequences of our choices. We can't always have His blessings if He doesn't always have our obedience. That would make Him our genie and not our God.

Today, let's remember the great God we serve and follow. There truly is no one like Him. He is God alone and worthy of our praise and devotion!

#ArmorUp!!!

DAY 68

Walk into New Beginnings

Good morning, brothers!

"For I command you this day to love the LORD your God and to keep His commands, decrees, and regulations by walking in His ways. If you do this, you will live and multiply, and the LORD your God will bless you and the land you are about to enter and occupy" (Deuteronomy 30:16).

While the Lord's love is unconditional, His blessings are not! Many people tend to miss this fact. They will say things like, "if God is so loving, then why doesn't He bless us all the time?"

As parents, we all love our children and want to bless them. However, will we give them things they have shown us they can't handle? God looks at us the same way. Our actions indicate to Him whether we are ready for His blessings or not. God has blessings with our name on it. However, He won't deliver them until we are ready to receive them. We need to stop blaming God for not blessing us when we won't obey His conditions.

We need to take responsibility for our actions and do something about it. Repent—turn away from our way and turn to God's way. Stay on His path and watch how things change. The Lord is not a genie waiting to grant all our wishes. He is a loving King looking to bless His loyal subjects. If we want to experience the blessings of the Lord, then we must choose to be obedient, unconditionally.

#ArmorUp!!

Represent the Lord

Good morning, brothers!

"And whatever you do or say, do it as a representative of the Lord Jesus, giving thanks through Him to God the Father" (Colossians 3:17).

We are representing the Lord to others, whether we want to or not. As William J. Toms has said, we "...may be the only Bible some person ever reads." So, what we say and do is what people attribute to Christ because we call ourselves Christians.

Now, this is not meant to add pressure to our lives. None of us are perfect, nor will we be. But our attitude and demeanor should always be pursuing Jesus. Our desire should be to live as Jesus lives and love as He loves. We need to be set apart for God's purpose and to pursue God's will. Because we are human, we will be imperfect. How we respond to our mistakes is what matters. We don't need to wallow in the muck when we fall into it. We know Who to go to for cleansing. We can find our perfection is Jesus!

#ArmorUp!!!

Jesus: Our Measuring Stick

Good morning, brothers!

"This is a trustworthy saying, and everyone should accept it: 'Christ Jesus came into the world to save sinners'—and I am the worst of them all" (1 Timothy 1:15).

Paul flipped the script on this one. People try to profess how great they are based on their accomplishments or how they measure up to other people. Paul's measuring stick here is different. He measures himself to Jesus and observes he is way off the mark!

Who is our measuring stick? Is it our job? The car we drive? How successful we (or others) think we are? Paul had accomplished many things people in his world would have been envious of. But, when he met Jesus, all that paled in comparison. Let Jesus be our measuring stick and not the world! We need a Savior, but we also need to follow our Lord!

#ArmorUp!!!

Remove the Weeds

Good morning, brothers!

"So get rid of all the filth and evil in your lives, and humbly accept the word God has planted in your hearts, for it has the power to save your souls" (James 1:21).

We let the weeds of the world choke the life out of the Word God planted with us. Sin grows so high that we can't see God's Word. It becomes so loud that we can't hear God calling us. Sin becomes so heavy that we can't carry the burden, and we stop moving forward toward God's calling. The solution?

Bring it to Jesus! Cast all your cares upon Him. Take His yoke on and learn of Him. Walk in His Word! Let's live by what God says and not by what history, culture, or tradition dictate. Victory is ours. We just need to do some weed whacking!

#ArmorUp!!!

Let the Lord Fight the Battle

Good morning, brothers!

"The LORD Himself will fight for you. Just stay calm" (Exodus 14:14).

When we are not calm, it is difficult to make good decisions. Many times, people will ask, "why did you do that?" And the response back is, "I was nervous" or "it was a rash decision." God is on the side of His children. There is no need to get anxious or worry. We can't allow nervousness to dictate our responses to situations. We must stay calm. We must focus on the Lord and trust He will do what He promises. Most importantly, we must invite the Lord into our situations and hand over the reins.

What a powerful reminder this is! When we surrender control to the Lord, He will fight the battle for us. His strategies may not always align with our expectations. So, we need to change our expectations! He Who sees the past, present, and future at the same time has a better viewpoint than us. We need to trust Him and follow His lead. Let's allow the Lord to fight our battles. He fights from victory while we are always looking for victory. We can leave the battle in His hands and watch what happens!

#ArmorUp!!!

The Lord Is with You

Good morning, brothers!

"For I hold you by your right hand—I, the LORD your God. And I say to you, 'Don't be afraid. I am here to help you'" (Isaiah 41:13).

The Lord God Almighty is present with us, wherever we are or whatever we're going through! But, even better, He knew about it before it happened! He already has a plan for us.

The question is not can He help, but are we willing to trust His help? We don't need to feel His presence for Him to be there. He just is! God will be God in our lives if we let Him. Can we do that? Can we let the Sovereign Lord rule in our lives? Let's allow His sovereign will to be done today!

#ArmorUp!!!

There Is Nothing Like Our Lord

Good morning, brothers!

"No one is holy like the LORD! There is no one besides You; there is no Rock like our God" (1 Samuel 2:2).

There is no one or nothing in the same category as our God! He alone is the true and living God. He is the same yesterday, today, and forever. But we try to put things in His place. We try to find our joy and comfort in our pleasures, possessions, or our position. These things can change on a whim, but God's consistency is what we can rely on. There is no peace, security, or longevity in any of those things.

Anything we compare to Him can't (and won't) measure up! He alone is worthy of our praise. So, let's turn back to the Holy One and leave these "hole-y" things alone. They can't fill or fulfill us!

#ArmorUp!!!

Watch Your Tongue

Good morning, brothers!

"Don't use foul or abusive language. Let everything you say be good and helpful, so that your words will be an encouragement to those who hear them" (Ephesians 4:29).

Proverbs 18:21 states the "tongue can bring death or life." We should, therefore, watch what we say. Like grandma used to say, "If you can't say anything good, don't say anything at all." We need to be careful with our words. We should seek to build others up and not tear them down.

I know sometimes I may say things and don't really hear what I'm saying. I need to be more conscious of how what I say will be received. Sometimes we justify what we say because it's true. Just because it's true doesn't make it right to say. We are instructed to "…speak the truth in love" (Ephesians 4:15).

Let's choose our words wisely today. Let's look to encourage others. Let the Lord do the reconstruction work on them!

#ArmorUp!!!

Simply Trust Him

Good morning, brothers!

"But the LORD watches over those who fear Him, those who rely on His unfailing love" (Psalm 33:18).

The Lord's truths are so simple! We look for complex thoughts and explanations, but the Lord speaks with simplicity. We need to simply rely on Him. He loves us and, when we put our trust in Him, He will protect us.

Many people think we should fear God because He will punish us if we don't. Two things are off about that thinking. One, God seeks to bless us. However, since He is holy, He won't dwell with sin. So, He distances Himself from sin and those who choose to dwell in it. Secondly, the fear the Bible speaks of is a reverence and respect for who He is, not for what He can do to us. That is the smokescreen the enemy uses to keep us wallowing in our sin. We tell ourselves, "you can't please God, and since He will punish you anyway, you might as well keep doing it."

True love doesn't hurt! And it never fails! Respect the Lord for who He is today. Let's take the Lord seriously. When we sin, we need to confess it, repent, and keep it moving (away from sin). Let's determine to seek His face and put our trust in Him. We won't be disappointed!

#ArmorUp!!!

Put the First Things First

Good morning, brothers!

"Seek the Kingdom of God above all else, and live righteously, and He will give you everything you need" (Matthew 6:33).

The world tells us, "don't put our eggs in one basket." We are encouraged to place our hope in many things. God is in the blessing business. However, He will only bless those who seek Him first. We have to place our trust in Him and Him alone.

The world is imperfect and so is everything in it. Everything and everybody can fail us at some point. Why place our faith in someone or something that fails and ignore the One Who never fails? Let's not chase after the things that are supposed to make us happy. Let's pursue the One Who will give us joy! When we choose the Lord, we gain more than the world could ever give us!

Put the first things first! Our purpose, our motivation should be on the things of God. When our focus is on Him, then He will take care of the rest. We have our priorities mixed up. The devil smoke screens us with pleasures, possessions, and positions. We focus on chasing them before we focus on God! Jesus is all we need! It's time for us to refocus!

#ArmorUp!!!

Endure Hardness

Good morning, brothers!

"Yet what we suffer now is nothing compared to the glory He will reveal to us later" (Romans 8:18).

We have all heard before the adage "short term sacrifices yield long term rewards." Paul's word to the Romans supports that statement. The world tries to convince us to pursue things that leave us empty once we get them. It wants us to take the easy way of life.

The Lord wants us to face the challenges of life. He wants us to "endure suffering" (2 Timothy 2:3). We will face trials and obstacles on this road. The Lord wants us to go through them. The men we become as we face these trials will be better than the men we are. This is true, however, only when we look to the Lord. No victory is sweeter than the one we get when we know we have obeyed the Lord! That confirmation of our faith feels wonderful!

Let's stop seeking worldly counsel for the spiritual life we are living. A map of Europe won't help us navigate America. How can worldly advice help us spiritually? Seek the Lord!

#ArmorUp!!!

DAY 79

Go through the Deep Waters

Good morning, brothers!

"When you go through deep waters, I will be with you. When you go through rivers of difficulty, you will not drown. When you walk through the fire of oppression, you will not be burned up; the flames will not consume you" (Isaiah 43:2).

Notice the Lord doesn't say "if"! The Lord is telling us that we will experience difficulties. He is telling us that when we go through difficult days, we will prevail. We WILL GO THROUGH! We shouldn't be surprised when we experience hard times. They are coming. However, we have no need to fear them because the Lord is with us! Our difficult days come to pass, not to stay. Remember, nothing catches our heavenly Father by surprise! Seek Him in those tough times.

When we choose to deviate from His plan, we prolong our stay in the storm. Let's stay the course and move at His pace and command. Paul tells us in Romans 8:37, "overwhelming victory is ours through Christ, who loved us." Let's face our difficulties with the confidence in knowing the Lord is with us, and He will guide us through them.

We must keep our eyes fixed on Him and trust His plan. Quote His Word back to Him, and watch what He does! Seek Him! Trust Him! Walk through it into victory!

#ArmorUp!!!

Be Still and Know

Good morning, brothers!

"Be still, and know that I am God! I will be honored by every nation. I will be honored throughout the world" (Psalm 46:10).

No matter how much experience men have, they immediately think they are experts at something! We constantly try to negotiate the circumstances and consequences of our lives to our benefit. The more we try, the more frustrated we can become. It's like that guy spinning plates on a stick. You are running around trying to give a little bit of attention to every plate. How much is enough? When is enough too much?

The Lord commands us to be still and acknowledge Him. He doesn't need our help. He needs our obedience if we want to glorify Him. Our stillness is not for Him, but for us. When we allow Him to take the authority, responsibility, and ordering of every detail, we find peace, joy, and success. Also, He is exalted as we praise Him for our deliverance. Let's hand over our worries and cares to the Lord. No one is better qualified to handle it all, for all of us, at the same time!

Moses told the children of Israel at the river to "stand still and watch the Lord rescue you today" (Exodus 14:13). Job was told to "Stop and consider the wonderful miracles of God" (Job 37:14). This act of submission is a sign to the Lord that lets Him do His thing! Whatever situation you have committed to God, when you stand still, He will take care of it. No matter how great or how small—trust Him with it and be still!

Let's allow the Maestro to control the symphony that is our lives and praise Him for the beautiful music He orchestrates!

#ArmorUp!!!

Be a Living Testimony

Good morning, brothers!

"Give thanks to the LORD and proclaim His greatness. Let the whole world know what He has done. Sing to Him; yes, sing His praises. Tell everyone about His wonderful deeds" (Psalm 105:1-2).

Our lives should be a living testimony to the greatness of our God. God has intervened in our lives in so many ways. How do we show Him our thankfulness? It's not just about saying how thankful we are. Neither is it about bragging to others about how blessed we are. It's about passing along a blessing to others. Remember, we are blessed to be a blessing. We should pay it forward.

How do we represent Him to others? Do we try to hide or deny His very existence? Our testimony is God's calling card to the world around us. What kind of representation do we give Him? Let's tell of His greatness!

#ArmorUp!!!

Good Doesn't Always Mean Blessed

Good morning, brothers!

"Can anything ever separate us from Christ's love? Does it mean He no longer loves us if we have trouble or calamity, or are persecuted, or hungry, or destitute, or in danger, or threatened with death?" (Romans 8:35).

The New Living Translation version has given me a new perspective on this verse. People think that because they have success, they have God's blessings on their life. However, Paul is saying the opposite isn't true.

So, take heart, dear brothers! Hardship is not a sign of God withdrawing His love! Don't see God in the midst of the storm. Allow God to see you through the storm! Don't fall for the "okie doke!" God always has and will always love you! Trust in Him and trust Him, especially when things get tough!

#ArmorUp!!!

DAY 83

We Need to Value the Present

Good morning, brothers!

"Teach us to realize the brevity of life, so that we may grow in wisdom" (Psalm 90:12).

Comic strip author, Bil Keane, said, "Yesterday is gone and tomorrow is not promised. Today is a gift. That's why it's called the present." We tend to take for granted the gift we have been given in today. We expect to have many more "todays" and therefore don't take advantage of the twenty-four hours God blessed us with.

We waste time doing things we don't enjoy and trying to impress people we don't know. This often causes us to neglect the things and people that matter most. Now is the time to reflect. How can I put more meaning into this gift God has given me? What changes do I need to make?

Let's invest our time wisely. Tomorrow is not promised. Let's make the most of today. Our time on this earth is limited. Let's focus more on making a difference than making a dollar! Let's seek God's guidance and follow His plan. When we do, He will make up the difference!

#ArmorUp!!!

True Friendship

Good morning, brothers!

"There are 'friends' who destroy each other, but a real friend sticks closer than a brother" (Proverbs 18:24).

Some "friends" are with you as long as it benefits them. They want what's best for them. A true friend is like family in that you can't get rid of them even if you wanted to! They are there no matter what the circumstances are and want what's best for you.

Thank God for those people in our lives who will tell us the truth and not just what we want to hear! They will weather a storm with us and stick around to help us rebuild the broken pieces of our lives. A true friend wants to see us be our best selves and will keep encouraging us until they see it. They are more "No, man" than yes men.

They are truly few and far between! We need to thank our friends who are like this. More importantly, we need to be friends like that!

#ArmorUp!!!

DAY 85

Stand Up for the Lord

Good morning, brothers!

"But it is no shame to suffer for being a Christian. Praise God for the privilege of being called by His name!" (1 Peter 4:16).

Alexander Hamilton once said, "If you don't stand for something, you will fall for anything." We have to stand up for what we believe in. The walk of Christ will be in direct opposition to the world system many times. We can find ourselves going in the opposite direction of friends and loved ones. We must stand firm and not yield to the pressures we face to follow them. We can't just "go along to get along."

The most popular path won't always be the right one, and the right path won't always be the most popular one! We must trust God's plan and stay on His path! When we stand up for the Lord, He will stand with us! Daniel and his friends did it! The apostles did it, and we can too! The pain we suffer for following our paths far outweigh any that we can, will, or have experienced for following Christ. Life is better with Jesus than without Him!

#ArmorUp!!!

With God, All Things Are Possible

Good morning, brothers!

"Jesus looked at them intently and said, 'Humanly speaking, it is impossible. But with God everything is possible'" (Matthew 19:26).

When we look at our circumstances with our human abilities, we see limitations. When we see our circumstances from God's perspective, we see limitless possibilities. We have heard in the hymn with the same name by Ira F. Stanphill, that "God can do anything but fail." Many times, it's just said as a platitude to comfort us when we are faced with a difficult situation. The question is, do we really believe it?

There are limits to what we can see and accomplish. The Lord wants us to come to Him. He wants us to rely on Him. God wants us to follow Him. He is the One Who sees yesterday, today, and tomorrow from the same perspective. He has spoken everything into existence and allowed us to rule over it. Shouldn't we want His advice? Shouldn't we desire His input? Shouldn't we follow His plan and walk in His footsteps?

The world tries to fool us into thinking we don't need God. No matter what we may think, He is still in control! His love has made provision for us to have a relationship with Him. Some people don't even realize the value of that! We need to stop relying on our limited viewpoints and the limits of others and turn to God. He as a victorious plan in place and is waiting for us to follow Him. Grammatically speaking, impossible becomes possible when we remove the "im." Spiritually speaking, the impossible will only become possible when I'm out of the way! Let's get out of the Lord's way, brothers!

#ArmorUp!!!

The Sharpness of the Word

Good morning, brothers!

"For the Word of God is alive and powerful. It is sharper than the sharpest two-edged sword, cutting between soul and spirit, between joint and marrow. It exposes our innermost thoughts and desires" (Hebrews 4:12).

Wow! The Word of God goes straight to the source! It gets down to the "nitty-gritty!" The Word of God is precise and purposeful. It will accomplish everything the Lord has planned for it. It reaches every crack and crevice of our thoughts, actions, desires, and motives. It examines and reveals things we try to hide. We try to hide our intentions from people and sometimes from ourselves.

Why does it penetrate so deeply? So that God can remove anything that is not of Him and heal us! He is not trying to expose us to embarrass us. Like a surgeon, our Lord wants to get to the root of our disease and remove it so that we can live a full and productive life. Wherever sin is hiding, the Word will find it, expose it, and cut it away.

Are we willing to lie down on the Lord's operating table and allow Him to remove the decay of sin? Will we wait on Him to reveal and heal us? Do we see the need for His Word to go to work in our lives? God won't force us to be healed, set free, and delivered. He just makes His Word available to those who are willing. The Doctor is in! His Scalpel is ready! Next!

#ArmorUp!!!

DAY 88

Who Will We Invite into Our House?

Good morning, brothers!

"The thief's purpose is to steal and kill and destroy. My purpose is to give them a rich and satisfying life" (John 10:10).

There are two points of view diametrically opposed to one another. We all know that. But we must choose daily which side we are on. Who will we choose to follow? Who are we inviting into our house? A thief or a life-giver? It's not about what we say but what we do. Who will we yield to? Who will we follow? Who will we trust?

We all have experienced brokenness because of our past choices and can still feel the hurt of past experiences. Let's not repeat! Follow the Lord and watch what happens! See your life really bloom and watch others be blessed as a result! Yield to His will today!

#ArmorUp!!!

Put the Responsibility on the Lord

Good morning, brothers!

"I am counting on the Lord; yes, I am counting on Him. I have put my hope in His Word" (Psalm 130:5).

Let's put the responsibility on the Lord today. However, that requires surrender! We have to bring whatever concerns us to Him and leave it there. There is security in putting our hope in the Word of God. God has told us His Word is trustworthy. "It is the same with My Word. I send it out, and it always produces fruit. It will accomplish all I want it to, and it will prosper everywhere I send it" (Isaiah 55:11).

What other kind of guarantee do we need? My grandmother used to tell me, "If God says it, then I believe it, and that settles it!" No further argument is needed. God is the only One who can be fully trusted at His Word. Yet we are quick to doubt Him and put our trust in the word of man. Throughout time, we have seen God's Word hold true. We have also seen man's word fail repeatedly.

Whose track record are we going to trust? God's Word is truth. When He says it will come to pass, it will! Walk in God's Word. Trust in Him. There is no other hope we need and nowhere else we need to turn! We need to trust Him to send His angels to deliver His answers to us. It will come to pass! Let's put our hope in Him today.

#ArmorUp!!!

God's Plan for Us

Good morning, brothers!

"'For I know the plans I have for you,' says the LORD. 'They are plans for good and not for disaster, to give you a future and a hope" (Jeremiah 29:11).

This is one of my favorite verses! If you ever wonder if God thinks about you or what He wants for you, here is your answer. The caveat is we must align ourselves with His plan. We can't go our own way and ask the Lord to "bless our mess!" We have to repent and get back in line. God is not a genie Who is at our beck and call to bail us out of our poor choices.

He has a plan for us. We must follow that plan if we want the future and hope that coincide with it. There will be no compromise. We either yield, or we miss the mark. God wants what is best for us and has provided a way for us to receive it. Are we going to follow the plan? Are we willing to give up the driver's seat? Do you want a future with hope or hopelessness?

#ArmorUp!!!

About the Author

Ray is a husband, father, educator, deacon and former high school coach who has spent years challenging young men and women to reach their fullest potential. His passion for obtaining and sharing knowledge has been evident his entire life. He continues share both his passion for learning and for serving the Lord Jesus and seeks to encourage others to pursue both as well. Ray and his wife, Pamelyn have six children and reside in the Pittsburgh, PA area.

Printed in the United States
By Bookmasters